A Year of Shapes

Reinforcing shape concepts with
hands-on learning activities

by
Dr. Margery Kranyik

Art by
Debby Dixler

Computer Graphics
by
Jill Levine

FIRST TEACHER PRESS
First Teacher, Inc./Bridgeport, CT

ISBN   1-878727-02-8

Cover and Page Design: Gene Krackehl
Cover photo: Andrew Brilliant and Carol Palmer (taken at Westfield Child Center, Brockton, MA)
Design by Gene Krackehl

Edited by Mary Lee Johansen
Editorial Assistants: Jessica Rubenstein, Alicia La-France, Thomas Jenen
Art Editor: Debby Dixler
Typesetting and Layout: Anita Golton, Jeffrey Goldfarb
Manufactured in the United States of America

Special thanks to Lisa Schustak, Kathleen Koons, Donna Bird, the children and staff of Rainbow Montessori School, Madison, N. J., and Hillary and Scott Dixler.

Published by First Teacher Press, First Teacher, Inc.
P.O. Box 29, 60 Main Street, Bridgeport, CT 06602

TABLE OF CONTENTS

3 3189 00199 8378

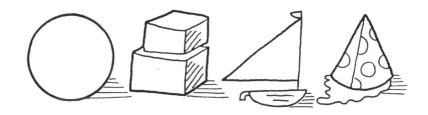

INTRODUCTION

Children are surrounded by shapes. Both home and school are filled with two-and three-dimensional shapes. Floor tiles and table tops are squares, windows and doors are rectangles, cans and glasses are cylinders, and fruit and balls are spheres. *A Year of Shapes* helps children explore two-dimensional shapes—circles, squares, triangles, rectangles—and three-dimensional shapes—cubes, cones, spheres, rectangular blocks . Active experiences with these shapes help increase children's knowledge of geometry and their ability to sequence, classify, build, predict and solve problems. An increased awareness of how to apply these skills will be helpful when they attend kindergarten.

A Year of Shapes takes a seasonal approach to activities and encourages children to explore shapes indoors and outdoors during different times of the year. This approach also allows you to integrate the actiivities into your existing curriculum. The activities—games, holiday motifs, art, movement and music projects, food preparation—allow children to work independently, with partners, and in small groups. Objectives for the activities include concept reinforcement (knowledge of shapes); motor development (movement, cutting, pasting, drawing), language skills (discussing, listening, following directions), and socialization (sharing ideas, taking turns).

To prepare for *A Year of Shapes*, survey your classroom and school area to locate objects having the shapes included in the activities. To help children with identification, have labels ready in the "shape" of the shape. For example, attach a square-shaped label to a record album cover or storage container or use a round label on a clock or jar cover.

As each activity uses inexpensive or scroungeable materials, invite parents to help keep you supplied. A list of items to save is included in the Letter to Parents on page 6. Be sure to ask early so you will have an ample supply of materials for each season.

Safety Precautions:

Careful supervision is necessary for any project included in this book, but especially the cooking projects and experiments. Only non-toxic supplies, crayons, markers, glue, paints, etc., should be used. Children should be taught to wash their hands after using the materials in each lesson and never to put anything but food in their mouths.

HOW TO USE THIS BOOK

A Year of Shapes can be used to supplement children's previous experiences with shapes. Each activity includes a lesson plan with objectives, materials needed, and detailed procedures. The activity sheet is reproducable. Although the process approach is emphasized, at the end of most projects, children end up with a product that can be observed, displayed in the classroom, and finally taken home.

What You'll Need:

This section provides a list of materials you will need to complete each basic activity. The supplies are inexpensive materials that are either common to most early childhood classrooms or throw aways from home.

Introduction:

Introduce each activity with a brief review of the name and characteristics of the shape. Ask questions such as: *"What is the name of this shape?"* Show picture of shape or object representation. *"Does it have corners or curves? Show us something in the room that is a (shape name). Tell us about something at home that is a (shape name)."* Repeat the name of the shape often as children do this activity.

What to Do:

In this section of each lesson plan, there are easy step-by-step instructions to help you guide children as they complete the basic activity. Children will need more or less adult help depending on their ages and developmental levels. All of the activities are open-ended enough to provide for much creativity.

Challenge:

Challenge activities are designed to stimulate the young learner who is ready to move a step beyond the basic activity. Challenges may be done as an immediate follow-up to your lesson or incorporated within your program at a later time.

Making Connections:

The activities in this section integrate the shape activity with other content areas. Extending the activity with a related song, poem, experiment, discussion, or art project helps reinforce the shape concept by building on children's previous experiences.

Books to Read:

This section links children's literature to each activity. Recommended stories relate directly to the shape activity or to the season in which the activity is presented.

Letter to Parents:

The Letter to Parents on the following page introduces your shape activities and encourages parents and children to explore shapes together.

Dear Parent,

Throughout the year, your child will be learning about these different shapes: circle, square, triangle, rectangle, cube, cylinder, sphere, cone, and rectangular block. These are shapes often seen outdoors. Buildings have shapes—some are square, others are rectangular and a few are round. There are shapes on the automobiles, trains, and airplanes. At home, your child sees shapes in tables, clocks, toys, and food.

Learning about shapes reinforces basic math skills that will be helpful for children to know later in school. Children see that some shapes have corners (square, rectangle, cube, triangle, rectangular block), while others have curves (circle, cylinder, cone). They begin to see similarities and differences and understand how to sort and categorize.

At school, your child will be doing many activities using shapes. Your child will have many experiences with two-dimensional shapes (circle, square, rectangle, triangle) and three-dimensional shapes (cylinder, cone, sphere, cube, rectangular block). The class will make toys, do art projects, play games, and prepare food—all related to learning about shapes.

Many of these activities need certain materials, many of which are scroungeable—throw-away items that you may have at home. If you can, please send any of the following items you have available to school with your child to help us with our supply of materials: empty half pint and pint milk or cream cartons; empty tubes from toilet tissue; foil; plastic wrap; scrap yarn; empty one-and two-pound coffee cans; cylinder shaped oatmeal boxes; ping-pong, golf, tennis, and small rubber balls.

You can help reinforce shapes while you are with your child. Look for shapes in pictures and ads as you read storybooks, magazines and newspapers and show them to your child. Talk about the many shapes you can see on houses and buildings as you walk around the neighborhood. Cut out cookies using circle, square, triangle, and rectangle shapes. Encourage your child to draw a basic shape and add other shapes to make a picture of a person, car, animal, building, or imaginary object. Ask them to name the shapes that they use. Visit your local children's library and find books that introduce shapes. Read the books together.

Shapes are all around us. Enjoy helping your child find them. Share the experiences and have fun!

Sincerely,

BODY SHAPES

OBJECTIVES:

- to introduce and reinforce the shape of a square, a triangle, a circle;
- to introduce the concepts of corners and angles;
- to develop body awareness.

This activity will help children experience the concept of corners, curves, and angles with their whole bodies.

What You'll Need:

Copies of Activity 1 • samples of a square, a triangle, a circle • red and blue markers or crayons.

Introduction:

Introduce the name and shape of a square, a triangle, and a circle as you hold up an example. Have children note corners, angles, and curves. Ask questions such as: *"Can anyone show me the shape of a corner? Can you show me the corners on the square? How many corners does a triangle have? Which shape is curved?"* Ask children to show you parts of their bodies that are like corners (bent finger joints, elbow of bent arm, heel) and curves (head, neck, chin, ear).

What to Do:

1. Provide each child with a copy of Activity 1 and a red and blue marker or crayon.
2. Have children identify corners and curves on stick figures. Direct them to mark corners with the red marker and to mark curves with the blue marker. Explain that the stick figures don't match real body outlines exactly.
3. Let children choose a partner. Help each pair imitate body positions on the Activity Sheet. Ask the partners to name each part of the body that is curved or that looks like a corner. Have children explain and demonstrate their choices.

Challenge:

- Encourage children to experiment in making circles, squares, and triangles using all parts of their bodies. Let children try this activity with a partner.

Making Connections:

- Challenge children, working with partners, to find five parts of their bodies that they can make to look like corners (e.g. bent elbows, knees, fingers). Ask them to see how many curves they can find or make. (Math)
- Help children identify the body parts they are using to make their shapes. (Science)

Book to Read:

Shapes, Shapes, Shapes by Tana Hoban (Macmillan)

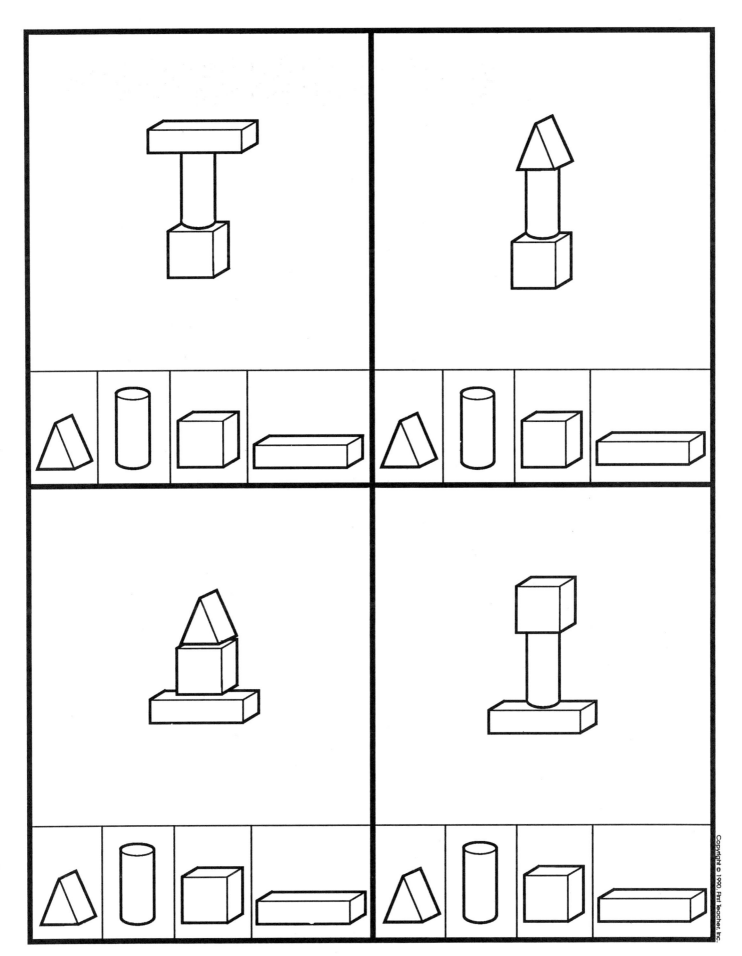

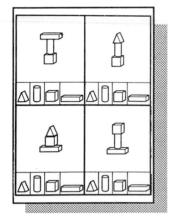

THREE-DIMENSIONAL SHAPE BUILDING

OBJECTIVES:
- to introduce and reinforce recognition of a cube, a cylinder, a rectangular block, a cone;
- to match actual blocks with pictured shapes.

Three dimensional shapes are difficult to understand unless you can actually feel the corners and curves and handle the shapes themselves. Help children move from concrete to abstract as they use a blueprint to create structures in the block area.

What You'll Need:
Copies of Activity 2 • enough large wooden blocks (cubes, rectangular blocks, cylinders, cones) in block corner for several children to work simultaneously • pictures of buildings, construction sites, construction workers.

Introduction:
If possible, show children a picture of a construction site or construction worker. Ask children how a builder knows what to do first, second, third, and so on when constructing a real building. Talk about how construction workers follow a plan when they build a building. Relate this to building with blocks in block area.

What to Do:
1. Provide each child with a copy of Activity 2. Explain that the Activity Sheet is a plan for making a building in the block corner.
2. Review the shapes of the blocks pictured at the bottom of the sheet and help children find matching blocks in the classroom.
3. Ask a few children at a time to take the Sheet to the block area and follow the plan to build the structure pictured on the Sheet. (You may want to demonstrate the placement of two blocks with each group, to get them started.)

Challenge:
- Ask children to describe their construction process.
- Using verbal instructions, have children build different structures. Give directions such as: "*Place a cube on a rectangular block. Put a cone on the cube. Place a rectangular block across two standing cylinders.*" Have children compare building from a blueprint to building from oral directions.

Making Connections:
- Wet your sandbox with water and have children make sand sculptures from sand packed and turned out from containers of different shapes. (oatmeal box, shoe box, paper cup, pail, cereal box). (Science)

- Encourage children to make shape sculptures in the art area using cardboard boxes of different sizes and shapes, empty paper rolls, and cone-shaped paper cups. (Art)

Book to Read:
Shapes by Fiona Pragoff (Doubleday)

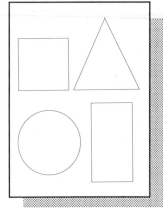

SPICED TWO-DIMENSIONAL SHAPES

OBJECTIVES:

- to introduce and reinforce recognition of a square, a triangle, a rectangle, a circle;
- to use the senses (smell, taste, touch) to reinforce learning.

In this activity, children use their senses of smell, sight, and touch to recognize basic shapes.

What You'll Need:

Copies of Activity 3 • samples of squares, circles, triangles, and rectangles • sand or assorted spices and/or seasonings (cloves, peppercorns, mustard seeds, ground cinnamon, nutmeg) or cornmeal and dried coffee grounds in small containers • glue • markers.

Introduction:

Show children examples of the basic two dimensional shapes, asking them to look for and point out curves and corners. Tell children that they can learn to recognize and identify these shapes by using their senses. If you are using spices for this activity, let children smell and taste them.

What to Do:

1. Provide each child with Activity 3. Have small containers of sand and/or foodstuffs, yarn, scissors, and glue available.
2. Have children trace carefully the outline of each shape with a marker.
3. Ask children to spread glue on the outline of each shape.
4. Have children sprinkle a seasoning, spice, or sand, etc. on the outline of each shape. Tell them not to worry if tactile material spreads around; it can be blown away from shape outline.
5. Have children display their shapes and point out curves and corners after naming each shape.

Challenge:

- Help children to cut out each shape on the Activity Sheet. With a hole punch, have children make a hole at the bottom and at the top of each shape. First demonstrate and then have them use yarn to attach the bottom of one shape to the top of another (through the holes), to form a chain of shapes. Make a yarn loop at one or both ends to hang up the shape chain.

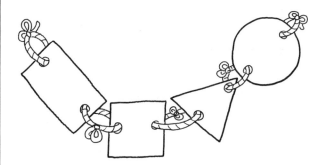

Making Connections:

- Read aloud the Shape Poem below.
  Rectangle, triangle, circle, square,
  We look for shapes everywhere.
  Corners and curves to help us know,
  That shapes are with us wherever we go.
  Have children add their own motions as you reread the poem slowly. (Language)
- Listen to "Circle, Triangle, Square" on the record *Learning Basic Skills Through Music Vol. II* by Hap Palmer (Educational Activities) (Music)

Book to Read:

Shapes by Tony Tallerico (Grosset and Dunlop)

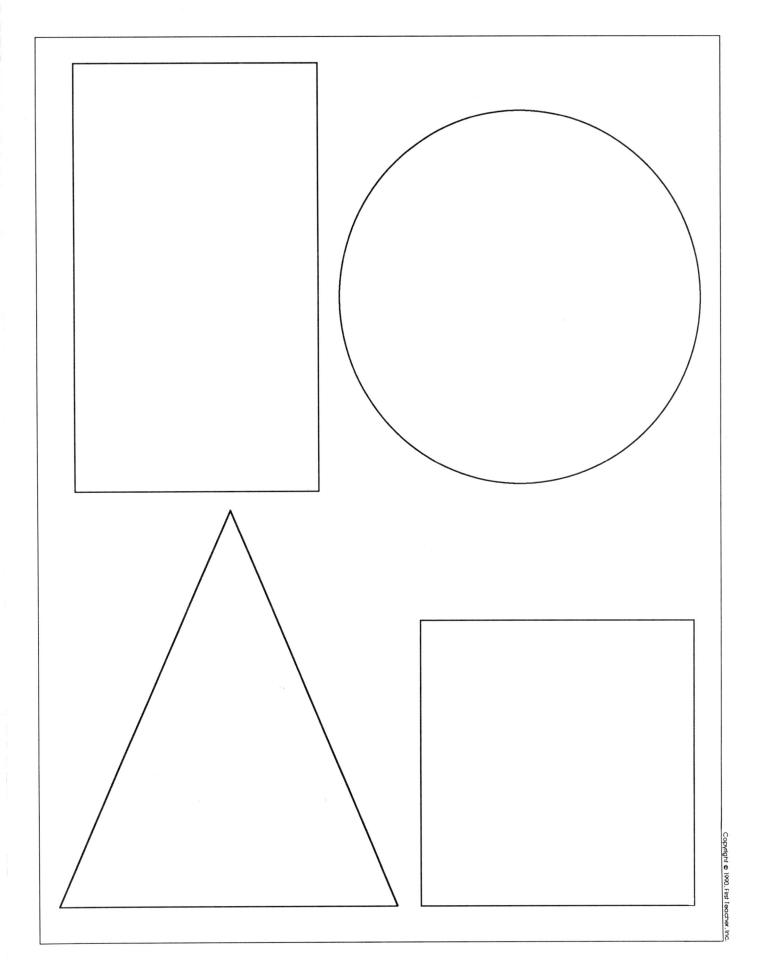

LEAF SHAPES

OBJECTIVES:
- to review and reinforce recognition of a circle, a square, a triangle, a rectangle, a corner, a curve;
- to sort (according to shape).

In this activity, children develop observation skills by collecting and matching leaves to shapes that look the most like their leaves.

What You'll Need:
Copies of Activity 4 • paper bags • glue • assorted leaves • shoe boxes • colored chalk or crayons.

Introduction:
Read a story or book about fall like *Down Came the Leaves* by Henrietta Gancroft (Thomas Y. Cromwell). Talk with children about leaves changing color and falling to the ground. Show children a variety of leaves. Ask them to tell you about them. Do any leaves look like triangles? Do some leaves have curves? Do any leaves have corners?

What to Do:
1. Take a walk with children; help them collect (in paper bags) fallen leaves of assorted colors. If this is not possible, have a variety of leaves or leaf shapes available.
2. When you return to the classroom, provide each child with a copy of Activity 4 and glue.
3. Ask children to place the real leaves they collected on top of similar shapes on their Activity Sheet.
4. Have children glue the leaf on top of the shape on the Sheet that it matches most closely.

Challenges:
- Encourage children to explore how the leaves feel—their texture. Have children tell you if the leaves are rough or smooth or bumpy. Have children choose a leaf that has curves, one that has corners, and one that has curves and corners.
- Have each child choose three leaves of the same variety and place them in size order from smallest to largest.

Making Connections:
- Fall Song (Tune: *Twinkle, Twinkle, Little Star*)
  Autumn leaves are falling down
  Whirling, twirling to the ground
  Yellow, orange, red, and brown,
  See them falling all around,
  Autumn leaves are falling down,
  Whirling, twirling to the ground. (Music)
- Help children make leaf rubbings by having them place leaves between pieces of tracing or typing paper. Have children rub over the paper with chalk. Spray with lacquer or hair spray. (Art)

Book to Read:
Marmelade and the Yellow Leaf by Cindy Wheeler (Knopf)

SPONGE PAINTING LEAVES

OBJECTIVES:

- to review and reinforce recognition of a circle, a square, a rectangle, a triangle;
- to develop creative expression.

Children will create very special works of art painting with shaped sponges using autumn colors.

What You'll Need:

Copies of Activity 5 • circle, square, rectangle, triangle shapes cut from sponges (several of each) • red, yellow, green, and brown paint • pictures and examples of fall foliage.

Introduction:

Discuss the changing color of leaves in the fall. Look at pictures. Show children leaves from outdoors. Read *Fall* by Joseph M. Parramon and Ulises Wensel (Children's Press) or other stories about leaves.

What to Do:

1. Provide each child with a copy of Activity 5.
2. Help children identify the drawing of the tree trunk without leaves.
3. Make available to each child shaped sponges and containers of paint. Help children to realize that the colors of the paint are the same as those of autumn leaves. Help children identify the shapes of the sponges.
4. Let children dip the sponges into the paint making sure that sponges are not too wet. Have children stamp the sponges onto the tree on their Activity Sheet to give the impression of leaves.

Challenges:

- Encourage children to print yellow sponge shapes over red ones to discuss what new colors they can create.
- Make extra copies of the Sheet to use at different seasons. Help children choose appropriate colors to use for each season and repeat the activity. You may also want to make round shapes for blossoms.

Making Connections:

- Read *In Fall* by Marie Claude Monchaux (Children's Press). Help children to learn one of the fall poems. (Language)

- Make simple color and shape patterns on paper using the shape sponges for children to identify, copy, and extend. (Math)

- Make a large outline of a tree on poster paper. Put out different art media and have children work in small groups to create fall trees to put up on the walls of the classroom. (Art)

Books to Read:

All for Fall by Ethel and Leonard Kessler (Parent's)
Fall Is Here by Jane Monecure (Child's World)

JACK O' LANTERN

OBJECTIVES:

● to review and reinforce the shape of a circle, a triangle, a square, a rectangle, a sphere;
● to develop creative expression.

Children will enjoy exploring the many uses of a pumpkin at Halloween and Harvest Time and will have fun carving different shapes in their Jack-O-Lanterns.

What You'll Need:

Copies of Activity 6 ● a large pumpkin ● knife (for teacher use) ● orange markers ● scissors ● black paint.

Introduction:

Hold a pumpkin up for children to observe. Let children feel its surface and tell you about its shape. With a marker, draw features in simple shapes on the pumpkin, based on children's suggestions. Guide them to include as many basic shapes as possible as features. Carve out the pumpkin face, saving the cut-out facial features and seeds for later use.

What to Do:

1. Provide each child with a copy of Activity 6 and orange markers.
2. Have children trace the outline of the pumpkin on the Activity Sheet with marker. Talk about whether the shape has corners or curves. Have children fill in the shape with marker.

3. Help children review the shapes on the pieces of pumpkin you cut out to make your Jack-O-Lantern face.
4. Have children in small groups dip the pumpkin shapes in black paint and print them on the pumpkins on their sheets to create their own Jack-O-Lantern faces.

Challenge:

● With children, examine the seeds you scooped out of your pumpkin. Dry roast the seeds in a warm oven. Let children taste them.

● Make additional copies of the Sheet. Have children paste the seeds from your pumpkin around the outline of the pumpkin on the sheet. Have them count the seeds on the outline. Then have children draw a Halloween picture in the outline.

Making Connections:

● The Jack-O-Lantern Song
(Tune: *Twinkle, Twinkle Little Star*)
  Jack-O-Lantern shining bright
  Smiling at me in the night
  Face with teeth and mouth so wide,
  Follows me from side to side.
  Jack-O-Lantern shining bright,
  Smiling at me in the night.
                    (Music)

Books to Read:

Best Witches: Poems for Halloween by Jane Yolen (Putnam)
Clifford's Halloween by Norman Bridwell (Scholastic)

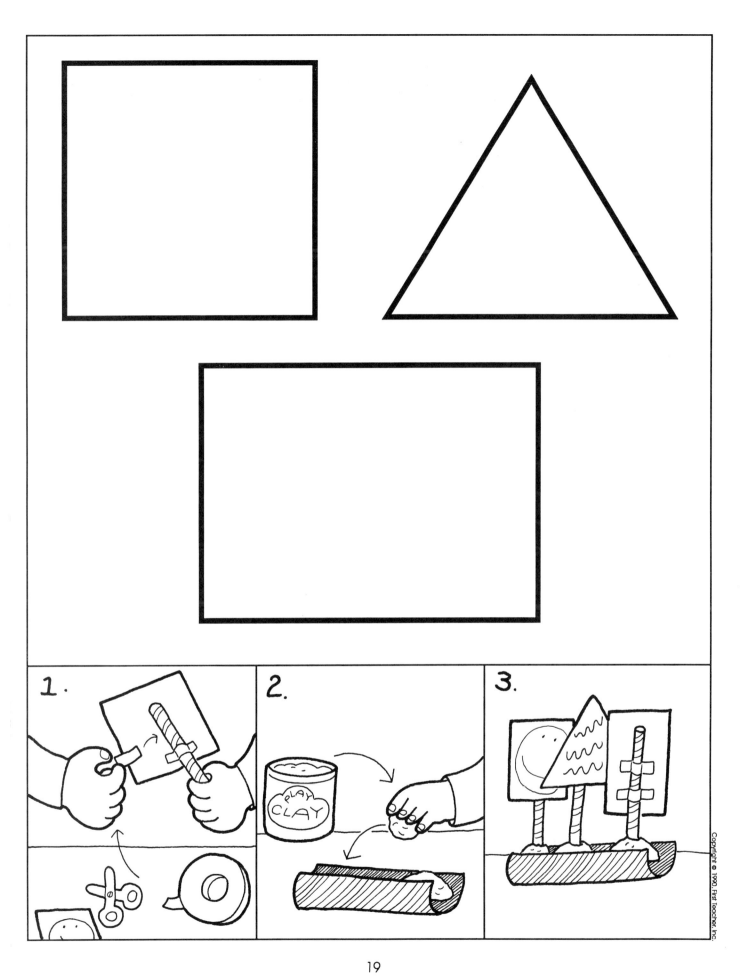

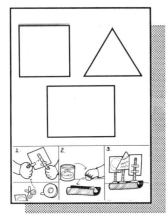

SHIP SHAPES

OBJECTIVES:
- to review and reinforce the shape of a sphere, a cylinder, a rectangle;
- to understand the difference between three-dimensional and two-dimensional shapes.

Celebrate Columbus Day by having the children create ships like the Nina, the Pinta, and the Santa Maria. This activity can also be used at Thanksgiving time to make a boat similar to the Mayflower.

What You'll Need:
Copies of Activity 7 • empty toilet paper rolls (to cut in half, lengthwise, for "ships'" hulls) • straws for masts (cut straws in half) • clay or play dough • crayons or markers • tape • scissors.

Introduction:
Discuss Christopher Columbus and why we honor him with a special day. Talk about the journey of his three ships to the new world. Show children a globe. Ask them to identify its shape. Then show children where Columbus traveled across the Atlantic Ocean, from Spain to the small island of Santa Domingo off the coast of the United States. You may wish to attach colored yarn to the globe and have children trace Columbus' route with their fingers.

What to Do:
1. Tell children that they are going to make ships that look rather like those that Columbus and his crew sailed in. Show children a toilet paper roll and help them to identify its shape. Then show them how you cut the roll in half lengthwise to make two semi-cylindrical sections. Give each child a section and explain that this is to be the ship's <u>hull</u>.

2. Provide each child with a copy of Activity 7, crayons or markers, and scissors. Help children identify the shapes at the top of the page. Have them decorate the shapes.
3. Have children cut out the shapes.
4. Give each child (or small group) straws, tape, and clay or play dough. Help children follow the directions at the bottom of the Activity Sheet to construct their ships.

Challenge:
- At Thanksgiving time, put yarn on the globe to show children the route taken by the Pilgrims crossing the Atlantic Ocean.

Making Connections:
- Talk about sailing. Have children who have been on boats share their experiences with the group. (Language)

Book to Read:
I Saw A Ship A-sailing by Cynthia Rylant (Macmillan)

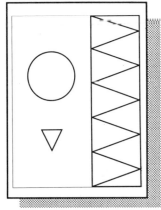

TURKEY TIME

OBJECTIVES:

- to reinforce recognition of a circle, a triangle;
- to reinforce creative expression through puppet-making.

Let children's imaginations soar as they create a turkey puppet to celebrate Thanksgiving.

What You'll Need:

Copies of Activity 8 • several good-sized turkey feathers (if available; if not, use illustrations) • six inch paper plates (at least one per child) • hole puncher • scissors • markers or crayons • glue.

Introduction:

Turkeys are a natural topic for discussion as you and your children prepare for Thanksgiving. Read a turkey story or sing a turkey song. Emphasize and talk about feathers— their colors, shapes, and textures. Have children examine real turkey feathers, if available; if not, use illustrations.

What to Do:

1. Provide each child with a copy of Activity 8. Have scissors, crayons or markers, paper plates, and glue available.
2. Help children identify the shapes on the Activity Sheet. Tell children that these will be the head, beak, and feathers for a turkey finger puppet they will make. Encourage children to discuss which shapes might make good body parts. (They will probably choose the circle for the head and the triangles for the feathers and beak, but don't discourage other creative ideas.) Have children add eyes to the shape they have chosen for the head and then color and cut out all the shapes.

3. Give each child a small paper plate. Talk about its shape. Ask children to glue the head shape to the plate and the beak shape to the head. Have children glue the feather shapes around the rim of the plate.
4. Help children make two finger-sized holes in the bottom of the plate. Demonstrate how the turkey becomes a finger puppet when you put two fingers through the holes as turkey legs.

Challenge:

- Have children make up little scenes with their turkey puppets.

Making Connections:

- Teach children this poem.
  Turkey, turkey in the yard
  You'd better run away.
  If you stay, you'll be our treat
  This Thanksgiving Day.
  (Language)
- If possible, visit a turkey farm. Learn about what turkeys eat, what sounds they make, how they move. (Science)

Book to Read:

Sometimes It's Turkey, Sometimes It's Feathers by Lorna Ballian (Abingdon)

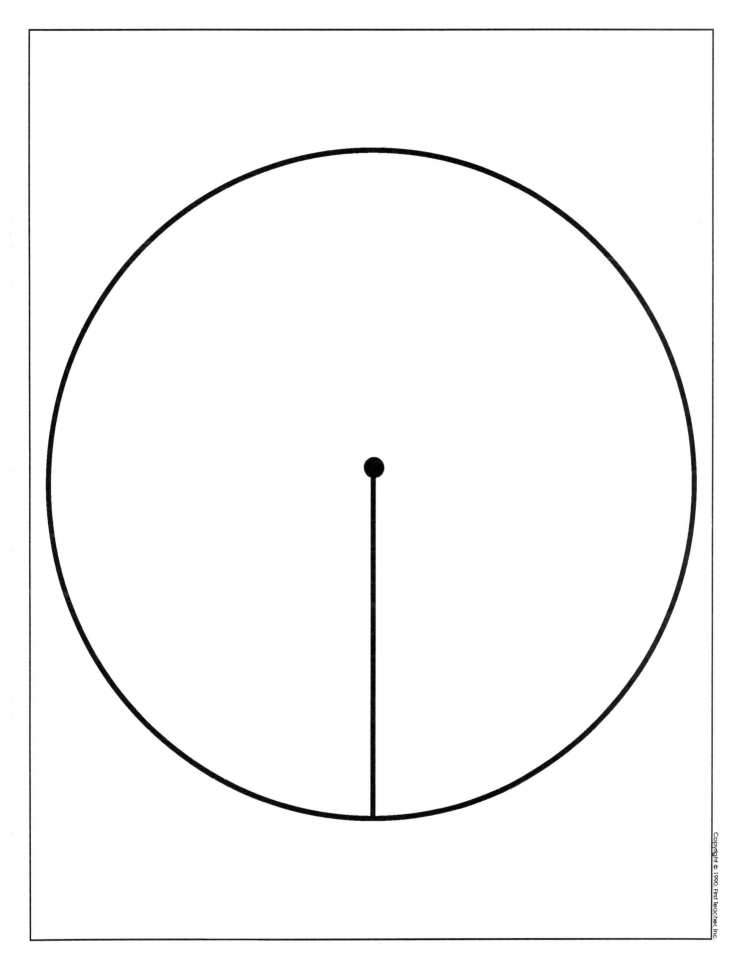

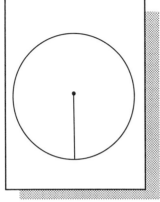

"SNOWBALL" TOSS GAME

OBJECTIVES:

- to reinforce recognition of a sphere, a cone;
- to review and recognize the difference between a circle and a sphere, a cone and a sphere.

Cold and icy winter weather often keeps children indoors. An indoor game made by children themselves can help release energy and stimulate imagination.

What You'll Need:

Copies of Activity 9 • scissors • cotton balls • colored markers • glue.

Introduction:

Ask children about activities we do outdoors in the snow (building forts, making snowballs, making snow figures, making snow angels). Show children a cotton ball. Ask them what the ball reminds them of. Help them, if necessary, with clues such as, "What is shaped like a ball and is white and cold?" Discuss the ball's shape. Then explain that they will pretend the cotton ball is a snowball and will make up a game to play with it.

What to Do:

1. Provide each child with a copy of Activity 9, a cotton ball, and scissors. Have markers and glue ready for small groups to share.
2. Help children identify the shape and then outline and color the circle with markers.
3. Have children cut out the circle and then cut on the line up to the dot in the center of the circle.
4. Help children overlap and glue the edges of the slit to form a cone.
5. Let children toss a cotton "snowball" into the air and catch it in the cone.

Challenge:

- Have children play a toss game with partners, tossing the "snowball" back and forth. Give them problem solving situations such as, *"Can you toss the "snowball" while taking a step backward?" "Can you toss and catch the "snowball" while standing on one foot?"*

- Have children make up other tossing games with partners or for small groups to play. Give partners and/or groups a chance to demonstrate their games and let other groups play.

Making Connections:

- Have children act out activities we do in the snow—skiing, skating, walking in deep snow, making tracks. (Creative Movement)
- Play the recording "Sleigh Ride" by Leroy Anderson (Boston Pops). Have children note sleigh bells and sound of horses' hooves. (Music)

Book to Read:

Happy Winter by Karen Gundersheimer (Harper and Row)

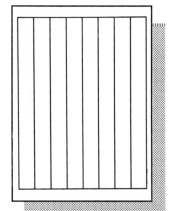

HOLIDAY CHAINS

OBJECTIVES:

- to reinforce recognition of a rectangle, a cylinder;
- to recognize and describe differences between a cylinder, a cone, a sphere.

Children will enjoy making this festive contribution to the classroom. Holiday chains make attractive ornaments for bulletin boards, windows, or a doorway.

What You'll Need:

Copies of Activity 10 • scissors • crayons or markers • glue.

Introduction:

Objects around us are made of shapes. One shape can also become another—a square when folded in half can become a rectangle; a circle can become a cone (as children saw in Activity 9). In the following activity, children will learn how a long rectangle can become a short cylinder.

What to Do:

1. Provide each child with a copy of Activity 10 and scissors. Have crayons or markers and glue available for small groups to share.
2. Help children identify the shape of the Activity Sheet. Then have them decorate and color each rectangular strip.
3. Have them cut out each strip (on the heavy lines). Help children identfiy the shape of the strips they have just cut out.
4. Ask children to glue the ends of the first strip together to form a cylinder.

5. Have them loop and glue each strip through the previous one to form a chain. Join chains together for room or tree decorations.

Challenge:

- Make wreaths or trees from chain loops.

Making Connections:

- From different sized rectangles and squares of paper, cut out different sized squares and rectangles of paper. Let children experiment with making long and short cylinders with different diameters. Some of these can be strung on yarn.
- Brainstorm uses for real chains—bicycles, necklace, dog chain, skid chain, chain saw.

Book To Read:

The Very Best Christmas Tree Ever by B. A. King (Godine)

SWEET TREAT HOUSE

OBJECTIVES:
- to reinforce recognition of a rectangle, a cube, a square;
- to follow directions in sequence.

Holiday time is often the time for special foods. The Sweet Treat House is a variation on the traditional gingerbread house.

What You'll Need:
Copies of Activity 11 • clean, empty pint milk cartons • chocolate and vanilla chips • raisins • colored lifesavers • mini marshmallows (for Sweet Treat House decorations) • graham crackers • FROSTING INGREDIENTS: 3 eggs, 1 pound confectioner's sugar, lemon juice; egg beater (hand or electric), bowl, plastic knives (for applying frosting). RECIPE FOR FROSTING: beat 3 egg whites to a frosty foam; add 1 pound of sugar slowly; add a few drops lemon juice; beat until stiff. <u>Note</u>: Do not make frosting until ready to use.

Introduction:
Read or tell your favorite version of *Hansel and Gretel*. Talk about the witch's candy house. If you are reading the story, show the children illustrations of the candy house. Write the ingredients and recipe for the frosting on the chalkboard to discuss with the children; emphasize the importance of following steps sequentially. Make the frosting with children's help.

What to Do:
1. Provide each child with a copy of Activity 11 and an empty milk carton. Talk about the shape of the carton.
2. Arrange decorations and plastic knives on a table for small groups to share. Talk about the shapes of the graham crackers—whole and halved—and other treats.
3. Help children follow the picture directions and attach graham crackers to the carton with frosting.
4. Help children frost the crackers on the carton and stick decoration treats onto the frosting. Have children tell you about the shapes they see on their house.

Challenge:
- Have children make up a story about who might live in their house. Write each story on a card to put with the house.

Making Connections:
- Have children listen to the music for the "Dance" from the opera *Hansel and Gretel* by Humperdinck. Let them make up movements to the music—dancing alone, in pairs, or in small groups. Ask children how the music makes them feel. (Music, Creative Movement, Language).

Book To Read:
Arthur's Christmas by Marc Brown (Little, Brown)

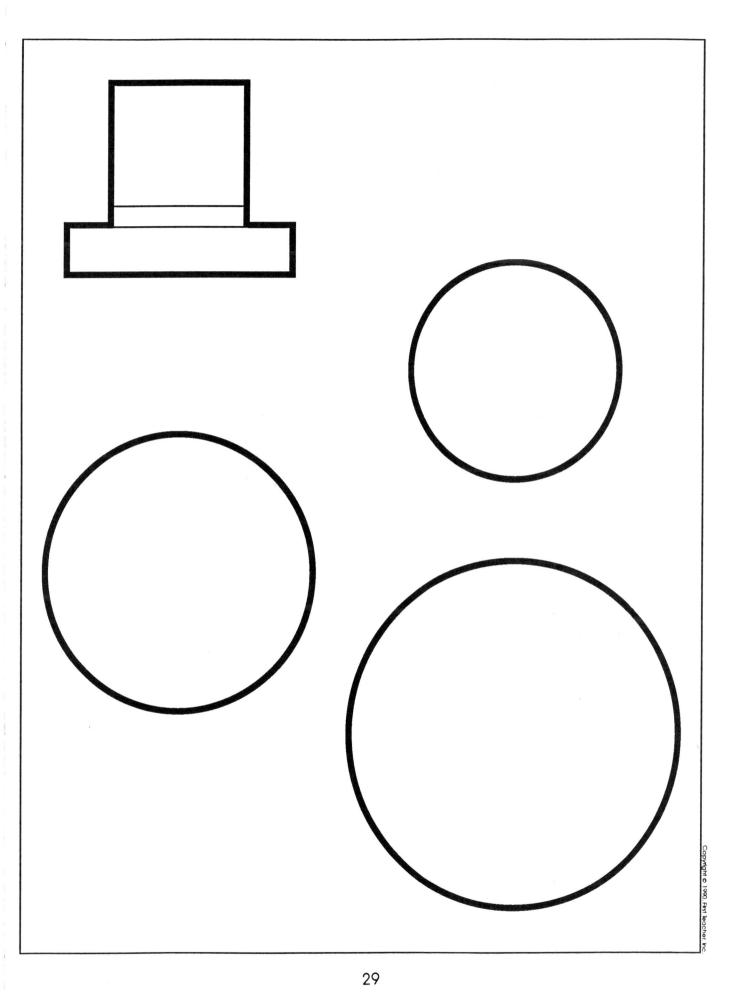

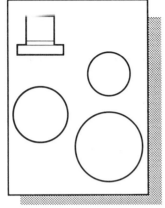

SNOW PERSON PUPPET

OBJECTIVES:

- to reinforce recognition of a circle, a cylinder;
- to reinforce creative expression through puppet-making.

A sunny day after a big snow can inspire the creation of both real and pretend snow people.

What You'll Need:

Copies of Activity 12 • scissors • glue • crayons or markers • empty toilet paper rolls.

Introduction:

Teach children the following poem:
GUESS WHO?
Guess who came into my yard one crisp and chilly day,
Looking for a special friend to sing and dance and play.
Wearing a hat and big warm scarf and buttons one, two, three.
It was a person made of snow who had come to visit me.
Talk about building a snow person and other snow sculptures outdoors.

What to Do:

1. Provide each child with a copy of Activity 12 and scissors. Arrange crayons or markers for small groups to share.
2. Help children identify the shapes. Then have them use their imaginations to tell which shape might make a good hat for a snow person. Have them color this shape. Ask children to draw circles for eyes and a mouth on the shape they would choose for the snow person's head.
3. Help children cut out the shapes. Demonstrate and then help children glue body parts together and add the hat and nose.

4. Give each child a toilet paper roll. Talk about its shape. Have children glue the snow person to a toilet paper roll to make the puppet rigid. Let children put their fingers through the hole in the roll to make the puppet move.

Challenges:

- Help children recite the snow person poem as they use their puppets.
- Encourage children to create their own snow person puppet story and use their puppets as they tell the story.

Making Connections:

- Play recording of song "Frosty the Snowman." Help children to learn the words. (Music)
- Have children pretend to be snowflakes. Pose problem solving questions such as: *"How would you move if you were a snowflake softly falling through the air? What would you look like if the wind suddenly started to blow? How would you move if you were slowly falling to the ground?"* (Creative Movement)

Book to Read:

The Snowman by Raymond Briggs (Little, Brown)

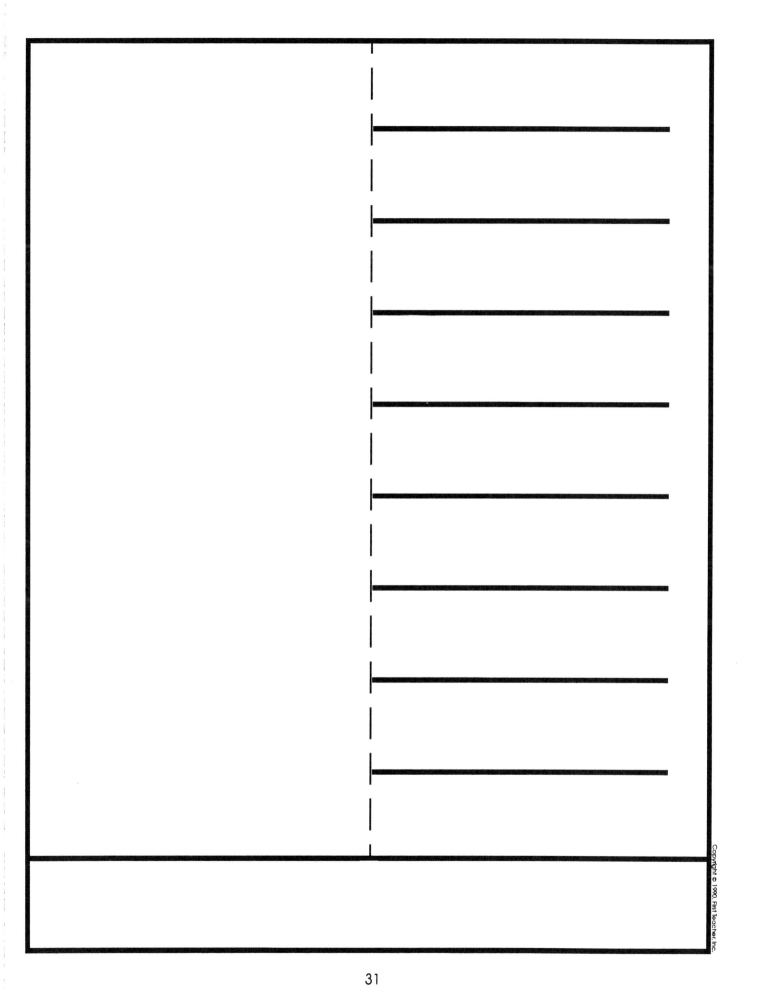

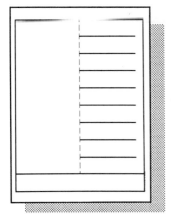

ORIENTAL LANTERN

OBJECTIVES:
- to reinforce recognition of a square, a rectangle, a cylinder;
- to introduce and reinforce knowledge of different cultures.

Introduce children to the midwinter Chinese New Year as they create oriental lanterns. Take this opportunity to explore several other cultures through their celebrations. Be alert to cultures represented in your school population and ask for parents" help in planning activities.

What You'll Need:
Copies of Activity 13 • scissors • tape • crayons or markers.

Introduction:
On a globe, show children where China is in relation to their home. Tell children about the Festival of Lanterns which ends Chinese New Year. A parade of lanterns is led by the traditional dragon through city streets to celebrate the Feast of the Full Moon.

What to Do:
1. Provide each child with a copy of Activity 13 and scissors. Arrange crayons or markers and tape for children to share.
2. Help children identify the large square and the long rectangle on the Activity Sheet. Have them color the shapes.
3. Have children cut out the square. Help children fold the square in half.
4. Demonstrate and then help children to cut along lines beginning at fold.
5. Have them open up the square and tape edges together (to make a lantern cylinder) as you demonstrate.

6. Help children tape the rectangular handle to top of lantern.

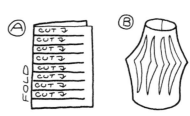

Challenge:
- Celebrate Chinese Young People's Festival by having children parade around the room with their lanterns. Let children use drums, cymbals, and finger cymbals for their music parade. Have the parade visit another classroom.

Making Connections:
- Help children to make a dragon head mask from a paper bag with streamers and pieces of colored paper attached. (Art)
- Explore ways in which the New Year is celebrated in other cultures. For example, in Bulgaria, children parade through the streets on New Year's Day carrying tree branches decorated with paper flowers. In Belgium, children write letters to their parents telling of the good deeds they will do in the coming year. (Social Studies)

Book to Read:
The Chinese New Year by Cheng Hou-tien (Holt, Rinehart, Winston)

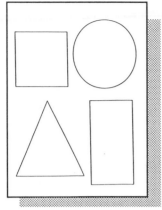

SHAPE OUTLINES

OBJECTIVES:

- to review and reinforce the shape of a circle, a square, a triangle, a rectangle;
- to practice problem solving.

In spring, you can have fun with shapes both indoors and outdoors now that the weather is warmer.

What You'll Need:

Copies of Activity 14 • ropes • measuring sticks of various lengths • branches • yarn • craft sticks • pipe cleaners • straws • glue.

Introduction:

Talk about shapes around us—indoors and out. Teach children the following poem.

> SHAPES
> *Point to a circle.*
> *Point to a square.*
> *Point to a rectangle.*
> *Shapes are everywhere.*

Encourage children to point to a variety of objects with distinctive shapes in the classroom and outside. Read the poem aloud several times.

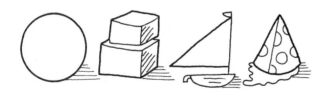

What to Do:

1. Provide copies of Activity 14 for each child. Have measuring sticks, ropes, and branches ready to take outdoors.
2. Help children identify the shapes on the Activity Sheet. Take children with their Sheets outdoors to flat surface—blacktop or grass.

3. Encourage children to take turns using the materials provided to make the shapes pictured on their Sheets. Have them identify each shape they make. After children have made one shape, ask: *"Can you use these same materials to make a different shape? Can you use different materials to make the same shape?"*
4. Return indoors and provide children with yarn, sticks, and pipe cleaners to glue on the shape outlines on the Sheet.

Challenges:

- While outdoors, have children collect natural items like twigs and grasses and outline the shapes on clean copies of the Activity Sheet.

- Have children make a line of shapes in a repeating pattern.

Making Connections:

- Have children play Guess-a-Shape. Encourage them to make up riddles such as: *"I'm thinking of a shape that has three sides (or three corners). I'm thinking of a shape that is made of curves."* (Language).

- Have children draw shapes in dirt or make shapes with ropes. Have them run, skip, walk to each shape as you or a child gives commands: *"Run to the square; hop to the triangle."* (Creative Movement).

Book to Read:

Snuffles House by Daphne Faunce (Children's Press)

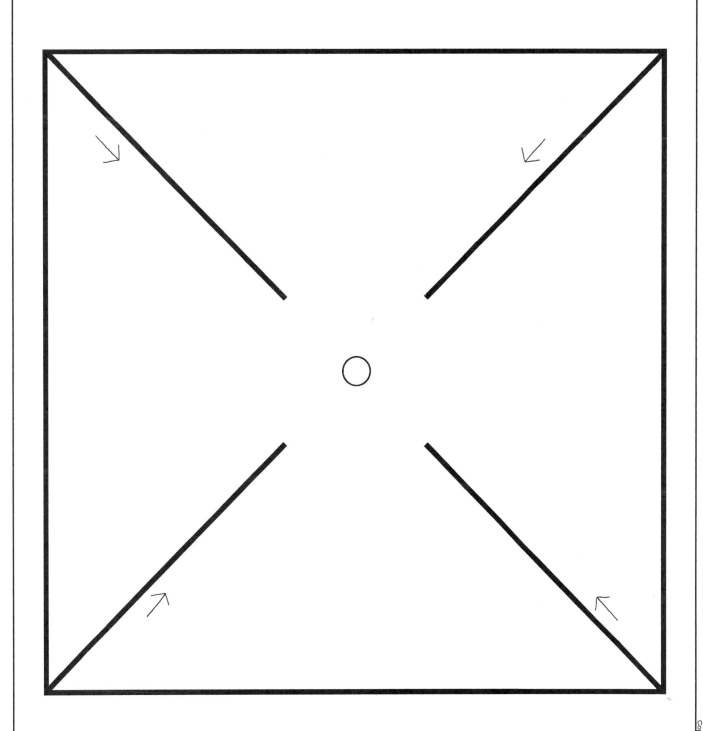

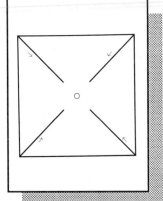

PINWHEEL

OBJECTIVES:
- to reinforce recognition of a square, a triangle.

Spring is noted for windy days. A pinwheel will help children see the wind blow.

What You'll Need:
Copies of Activity 15 • scissors •crayons or markers • tape • empty toilet paper rolls • paper fasteners.

Introduction:
If possible, read the poem "Who Has Seen the Wind" by Christina Rosetti. Talk to children about effects of wind, both good and bad. Discuss things we use to measure wind speed. Show children a pinwheel which you have made using Activity 15.

What to Do:
1. Provide each child with a copy of Activity 15, scissors, crayons or markers, an empty toilet paper roll, and paper fastener.
2. Help children identify the large square and count the corners on the outside of the square. Have children color in and then cut out the shape. Then have them cut along the heavy lines at the four corners.
3. Demonstrate and then help children fold the corners of the shape where there are arrows into the center (small circle) and secure with tape.

4. Help children push a paper fastener through an empty toilet paper roll and then through the center of the folded shape. Fasten loosely.

Challenge:
- Have children take their pinwheels outdoors to see if the wind will blow them.

Making Connections:
- Have children move like the wind. Ask questions such as: "How would you look if you were a leaf blowing in a gentle wind? How would you move if the wind blew hard?" Have children make believe they are leaves falling to the ground as the wind dies down. (Creative Movement)
- Show children pictures of old-fashioned windmills in Holland and modern ones also. Encourage children to pretend to be a windmill. Ask questions like: "How would your arms move if you were a windmill? What would you do if the wind blew hard? What would happen to you if the wind blew softer and softer until finally it stopped blowing?" (Creative Movement)

Book to Read:
Spence Makes Circles by Christa Chevalier (Whitman)

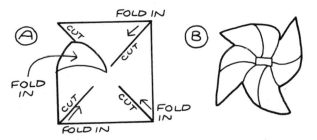

SHAPE DRUM

OBJECTIVES:
- to reinforce recognition of a cylinder, a circle, a rectangle;
- to develop and reinforce a sense of rhythm.

Celebrate spring with your own parade and play shape drums that children make themselves.

What You'll Need:
Copies of Activity 16 • scissors • crayons or markers • yarn • glue • colored and/or patterned paper • empty cardboard cylinders with lids like oatmeal boxes • dried peas, beans, uncooked popcorn, or pebbles • hole puncher • smooth wooden sticks (for beating drums).

Introduction:
Talk about drums. Let children examine a toy drum. Ask them to point out any shapes they see.

Teach children the following poem:
THE DRUM
The drum, the drum-a-rum-a-ta-tum-a-ta-tum.
I know a parade by the sound of a drum
A-rum-a-ta-tum-a-ta-tum.
The drum, the drum-rum-a-ta-tum-a-ta-tum.
Let everyone come and join in the fun
A-rum-a-ta-tum-a-ta-tum.

What to Do:
1. Provide each child with a copy of Activity 16 and an empty cardboard cylinder with lid. Punch hole on both sides of the cylinder so children can thread yarn through according to the picture directions. Talk about the shape of the box and the shape of its lid. Have scissors, glue, and crayons or markers available for groups to share.

2. Demonstrate how to make a drum following the directions on the Activity Sheet.
3. Help children make their own drums following the directions and using the materials provided.
4. Let each child demonstrate the sound of his drum.

Challenge:
- Play march music and have children form a parade keeping time to the music with their drums.

Making Connections:
- Teach children the following song:
TEN LITTLE INSTRUMENTS
One little, two little, three little instruments
Four little, five little, six little instruments
Seven little, eight little, nine little instruments
Ten instruments in the band.
Have children play their drum each time they sing a number. (Music, Math)

Book to Read:
The First and Last Animal Pet Parade by Mary Neville (Pantheon)

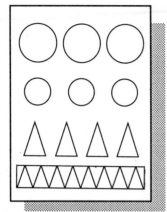

SHAPE BOUQUET

OBJECTIVES:

- to reinforce recognition of a triangle, a cone, a circle, and their differences;
- to reinforce the pleasure of giving to others.

May Day is a time for surprising a friend or family member with flowers. Shape bouquets can be a charming surprise for a child's special friend.

What You'll Need:

Copies of Activity 17 • markers • glue • scissors • six inch round doilies • pipe cleaners • hole puncher.

Introduction:

Tell children a story of May Day tradition, leaving a basket of flowers on a friend's door-step. Discuss the word "surprise." Have children ever had a surprise or created a surprise for someone else? Introduce this activity as a surprise children can make for a favorite friend or family member.

What to Do:

1. Provide each child with a copy of Activity 17, scissors, and crayons or markers. Have glue, pipe cleaners, and a hole puncher ready for small groups to share.
2. Help children identify each shape. Tell them that they are going to use the shapes to make flowers to give as a surprise to a friend. Have them trace around the shapes with a colored marker. Then have them color the shapes.
3. Let children cut out each shape. Have children glue the shapes together to make flowers. (Some children may choose to use triangles for leaves instead of petals.)
4. Help children punch a hole in the center of each flower and attach a pipe cleaner stem.

5. Give each child a doily. Discuss its shape. Put a large dot in the center of each doily and a cutting line from the edge to the center dot. Have children cut doily to the dot in the center.
6. Have them glue overlapped edges of doily together to form a cone. Have children place their flower bouquets into the cones, pushing pipe cleaner stems through the centers.

Challenge:

- Plant flower seeds in your classroom and chart their growth progress. Plant a flower outside the classroom in the soil. Have children note and measure its growth.

Making Connections:

- Play "Waltz of the Flowers" from *Nutcracker Suite* by Tchaikovsky. Have children make up movements to perform to the music. (Music, Creative Movement)
- Talk about how flowers grow—some from bulbs, others from seed. Encourage children to bring in magazine illustrations of flowers and plants. Talk about flower and leaf shapes. (Science)

Book to Read:

This Year's Garden by Cynthia Rylant (Macmillan)

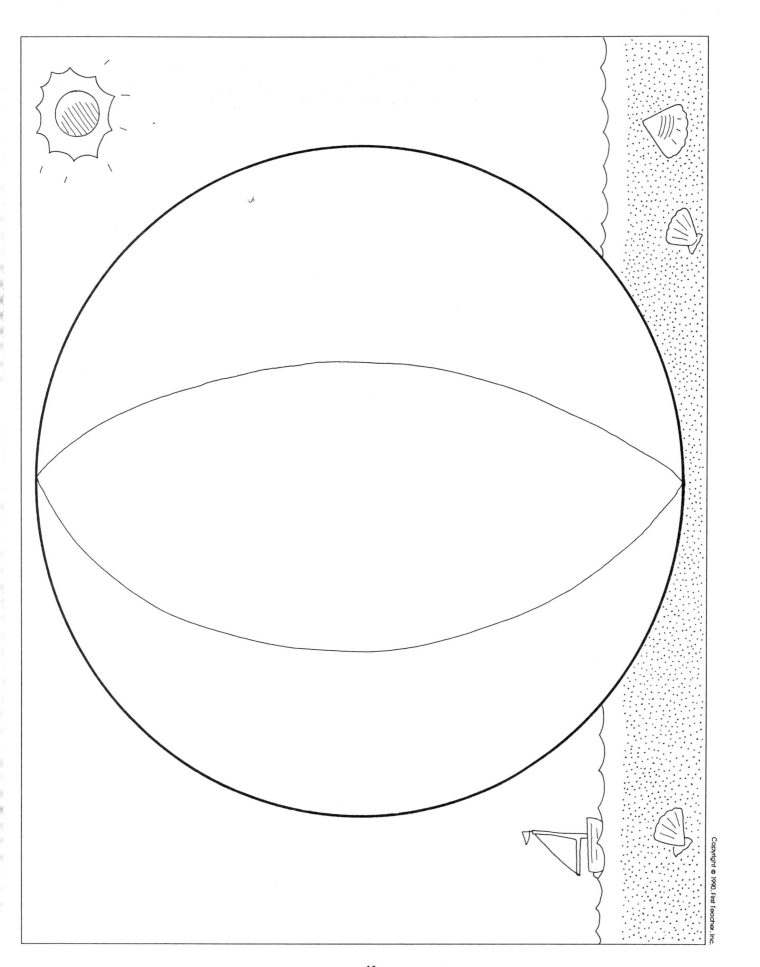

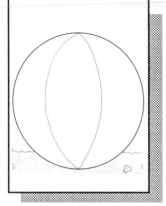

BEACH BALL DECORATIONS

OBJECTIVES:
- to review and reinforce the recognition of a sphere, a cylinder, a circle;
- to experiment with creating patterns.

Beach balls are spheres that are part of summer fun. Children will enjoy creating a colorful picture of a beach ball with circles printed from a variety of cylindrical shapes.

What You'll Need:
Copies of Activity 18 • scissors • paint in various bright colors • empty toilet paper or foil roll • straw • gift wrap roll • various sized cylinders • real examples or pictures of decorated beach balls.

Introduction:
Show children decorated beach balls. See what shapes children can identify in the designs. Encourage children to find any repeating patterns in the designs. Then talk about printing with shapes. Show children a cylinder, dip it in paint, and ask children what shape they think it will make when printed on paper.

What to Do:
1. Provide each child with a copy of Activity 18. Provide dishes of paint and cylinders of various sizes for small groups to share.
2. Help children identify the object on the Activity Sheet. Then have children dip the ends of various sized cylinders in the paint and print within the shape on the Sheet. Encourage children to make repeating patterns with sizes and colors of circles.

Challenge:
- Have children use balls of various sizes and textures (tennis, golf, Nerf) to make ball prints on plain paper. Show children how to dip a ball in a dish of paint and roll it on the surface of the paper. Have children describe each different print. Which was made by a large ball? A small one?

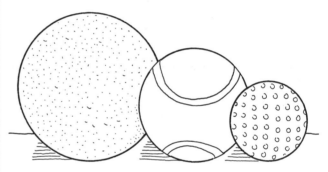

- Have children look at a partner's prints and see if they can tell which ball made the print.

Making Connections:
- Have children tell you about other sports they know that are played with balls. (Language)
- Provide an assortment of balls for children to sort (size, color) and categorize (indoor or outdoor play; team or individual sport). (Math)

Book to Read:
Blue Bugs Beach Party by Virginia Poulet (Children's Press)

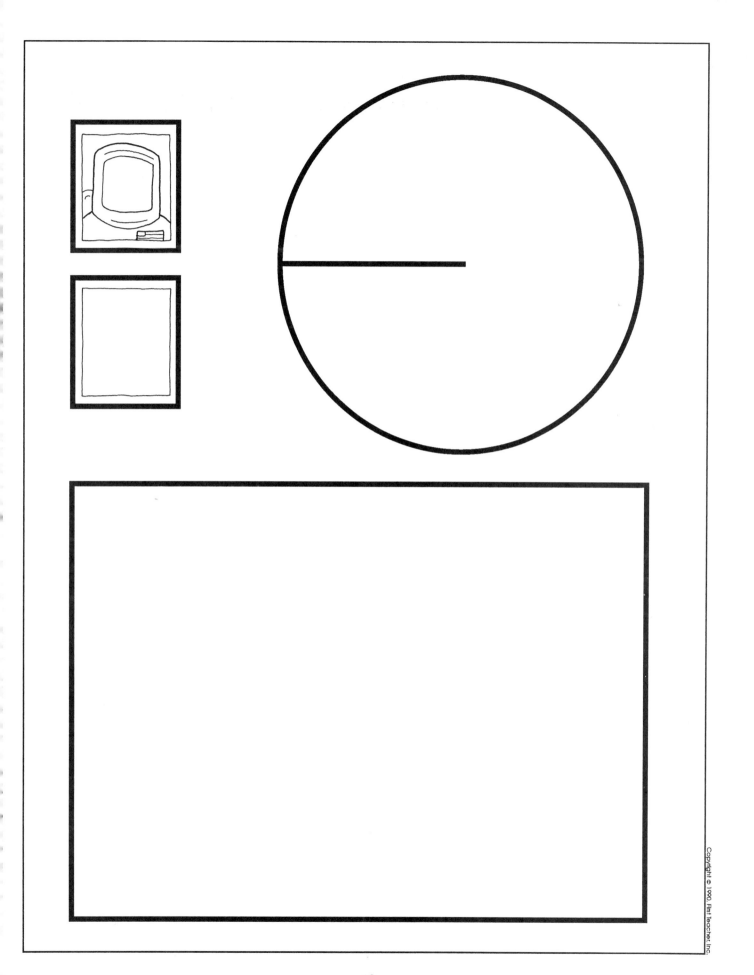

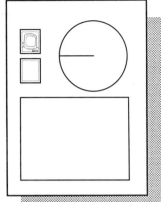

ROCKET SHIP

OBJECTIVES:

- to reinforce recognition of a square, a cylinder, a cone.
- to introduce and reinforce information about space exploration and rockets (shape, how rockets work, where they travel).

Summertime sparks special interest in the sky—fireworks, meteors, Northern Lights. In July we celebrate space week—a time to think about and explore outer space. Use this activity to blast off to a study of the sky or outer space, or use it anytime you want to have "far out" fun.

What You'll Need:

Copies of Activity 19 • scissors • markers • glue • empty toilet paper rolls.

Introduction:

Talk about Space Week. America's first attempt at space exploration was with the rocket. The first rockets were sent into outer space without people in them to explore what was there. Later rockets were used to launch astronauts into space. Today rockets launch space shuttles that orbit the globe and then land back on earth. Celebrate the week by introducing this rocket activity.

What to Do:

1. Provide each child with a copy of Activity 19, scissors, and markers. Have glue available for the group to share.
2. Help children identify the shapes on the Activity Sheet. Explain that these will be parts of their rocket ship (windows, doors, nose). Have children color the shapes. Encourage children to draw a face on the astronaut in the window and draw another face in the other window.
3. Ask children to cut out the shapes.
4. Have children find the circle. Demonstrate and then help them to cut on the line which goes from the edge to the center of the circle.
5. Demonstrate and help children glue the parts of the circle together to form the nose cone of the rocket ship. Talk about the shape they have created.
6. Give each child a cardboard tube. Have children identify its shape and compare it to the nose cone. Demonstrate as you have children glue the nose cone and other shapes to the tube to create the rocket with doors and windows.

Challenge:

- Invite children to tell you where they would lift off to if they could go any place they wished in a rocket.

Making Connections:

- Help children make a space mural that includes a moon and stars. Let children attach their rocket ships to the mural with tape. (Science, Art)

Book to Read:

Magic Monsters Learn About Space by Jane Belk Moncure (Children's Press)

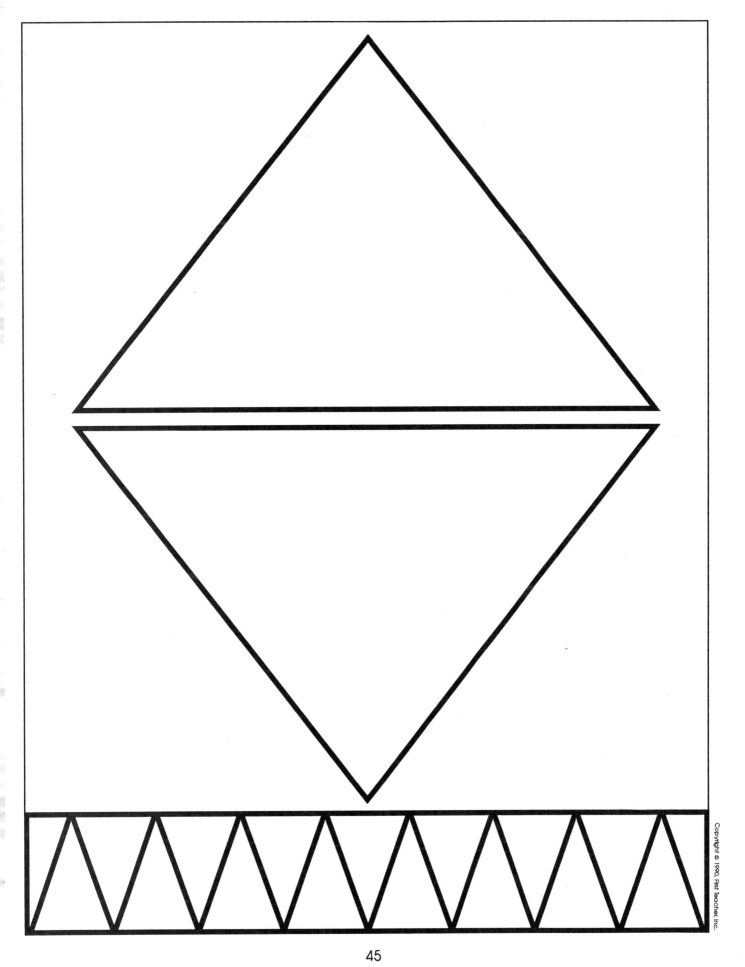

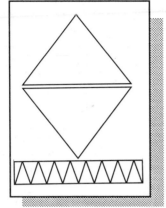

KITE

OBJECTIVES:

- to reinforce recognition of a triangle;
- to experiment with a kite to discover the effect of wind.

A breeze in a meadow or at the beach will help kites to soar and bring delight to children. And a kite can fly off the ground just by having a child run with it.

What You'll Need:

Copies of Activity 20 • scissors • markers • glue • string cut in four foot lengths • strips of crepe paper 1 1/2 inch wide • tape.

Introduction:

Teach children this poem:

MY KITE

On windy days I fly my kite
And watch it soar on high
It sails away, so far away
In the cloudless summer sky

Ask questions such as, "*How many of you have ever flown a kite? Where did you fly it? "What helped the kite to get off the ground?"* Explain to children that they will each make a kite and discover what happens when they run with it outdoors.

What to Do:

1. Provide each child with a copy of Activity 20 and scissors. Have glue, markers, string, and crepe paper available for groups to share.
2. Help children identify and then color the triangles, both large (for the kite body) and small (for the kite tail).
3. Ask children to cut out each triangle.
4. Demonstrate as you have children glue the large triangles together, base to base, overlapping slightly.

5. Measure and cut two feet lengths of crepe paper for each child. Demonstrate and then have children glue the small triangles to each side of the crepe kite tail. Leave a few inches between triangles.
6. Help children use tape to attach a string to one end of their kite and the crepe tail to opposite end. Go outdoors to let children try to fly their kites. Let them discover what happens when they run fast with their kite.

Challenge:

- Have children pretend that their kite is flying over their home. Ask them, "*What would your kite see? If you were holding on to your kite's tail, where would you like the kite to take you?*"

Making Connections:

- Take a walk outdoors (in a park, on a beach, in the woods) to collect stones, leaves, shells, etc. Ask children to match their found objects to shapes they see and know in the room. Draw different shapes on the chalkboard and have children take turns matching their objects to the shapes. (Math).

Book to Read:

Wind Blew by Pat Hutchins (Macmillan)

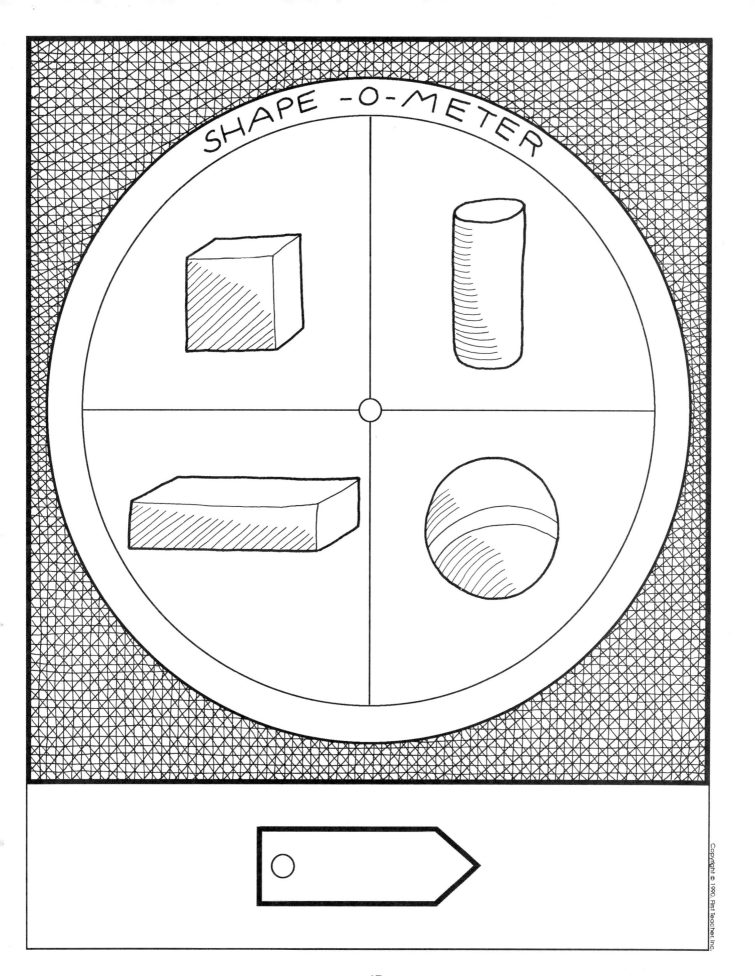

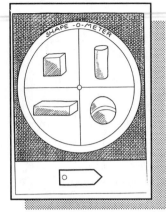

SHAPE-O-METER

OBJECTIVES:

- to reinforce recognition of a cone, a sphere, a cube, and a rectangular block;
- to reinforce recognition and naming of the specific shapes of common objects.

Summer is a season for games—outdoors if the sun shines, and indoors if it rains. This game with shapes can be extended and adapted to include a variety of shapes and colors.

What You'll Need:

Copies of Activity 21 • magazines •paper fasteners • scissors • markers • board game-spinner.

Introduction:

Use magazine pictures or common objects as examples to talk about and compare basic shapes. Show children a board game spinner and demonstrate how it works. Tell them that they will make a spinner called a Shape-o-meter and play a shape game with it.

What to Do:

1. Provide each child with a copy of Activity 21. Have paper fasteners, scissors, and markers available.
2. Help children identify each shape in the wheel. Have children trace around the edge of the wheel and then color the shapes in the wheel and the arrow pointer.
3. Have children cut out the arrow pointer.
4. Demonstrate and then help children attach the arrow to their Shape-o-meter with a paper fastener. Show them a board game spinner as a model.
5. Show children a collection of everyday objects with observable basic shapes corresponding to those on the Shape-o-meter. Have children identify the shape of

the object by moving the arrow to the matching shape.

Challenges:

- Take a walk outdoors. Have children use their Shape-o-meter to identify the shapes of different objects.

- With partners taking turns, have one child select a shape on the Shape-o-meter for the other child to find in the room.

Making Connections:

- As you turn the arrow to each shape on a Shape-o-meter, have children try to make that shape with parts of their body. (Creative Movement)
- Using a large piece of blank paper, help children make another Shape-o-meter. Let them draw different colored circles on the wheel. Then let children take turns turning the arrow to a color while another child finds an object of the same color. (Art)

Book to Read:

Flap Your Wings and Try by Charlotte Pomerantz (Greenwillow)